keiron higgins

Rebel Without A Prose: The Writings Of A Working Class Fake

Punk Poetry & Urban Haligonian Tales

Copyright © 2017 keiron higgins

Publisher: tredition, Hamburg, Germany

ISBN
Paperback: 978-3-7323-9010-6

Printed on demand in many countries

*These poems are dedicated to the memory of my father,
Cornelius Whylie and my mother, Tina Sheldrake.*

KEIRON HIGGINS

REBEL WITHOUT A PROSE: THE WRITINGS OF A WORKING CLASS FAKE

punk poetry and urban Haligonian tales.

© 2017 Keiron Higgins
Cover, Illustrations: Keiron Higgins

Publisher: tredition GmbH, Hamburg, Germany

ISBN
Paperback   978-3-7323-9010-6

Contents:

Introduction:

Keiron Higgins is a 30 something "Punk Poet" (a term he's actually come to live with during performance) from the aisle of Halifax, West Yorkshire. Keiron started doing spoken word as a secondary outlet to music production in 2013 after seeing the likes of close friend and fellow punk poet Cayn White over the years, and been spurned on by attending Genevieve Walsh's (one member of the up and coming poet collective, FIRM OF POETS) first spoken word night.

calling himself a proclaimed shape shifter, and a hard bitten poetic punk performing rapid fire rhyming tongue-fulls of lyrical eccentricity to point out the good and bad things in his life, in topics battles dyspraxia, oppression, depression and any given alcoholic beverage at hand.

Citing himself as been a cross between John Lydon, Travis Bickle and Mickey Pearce, In 2014 He has has graced (or "invaded") the spoken word stage at Rebellion Punk Festival in Blackpool, as a warm up act for when the main performers where about to perform.

In 2015, he released his first chapbook **Keiron Higgins: PUNK POET AND CUNNING-LINGUIST** and has become the co-host/compere for Genevieve Walsh's Spoken Weird night based in Halifax. In 2016 he has supported the likes of Attila The Stockbroker, Steve Ignorant's Slice of Life, Evil Blizzard, and ex. Stiff Little Finger member Henry Cluney. His prolific CV as of supporting poet for acts and a regular at open mic nights in Sowerby Bridge is often welcomed with praise from his peers and headlining acts.

An Interview With Keiron Higgins: From Hull To Halifax by KL WHYLIE.

Today is a sunny day in Halifax, but this mood is set to be darkened as I await the appearance of a certain poet named Keiron Higgins. Keiron, aged 30 has been a spearhead of poetic performance in his hometown of Halifax for at least 4 years now, with a CV that boasts supporting the likes of ex Crass member Steve Ignorant and the infamous Attila The Stockbroker. Today I sat down with him to get the facts behind his often eccentric persona.

Q: Tell us about your history.

KH: as my opening poem "I am" states, I am born of a mixed race descent, specifically Jamaican/Irish. My grandfather of my dad's side came to Halifax in the 60s and was born in Rockwell, Kingston Jamaica. He saw the first movement of Ska, one of my musical loves. My grandfather on my mother's side came from a large Irish family but we never met, as he passed on at the age of 50. There are stories in the 60's he played for Bradford Northern (now the Bradford Bulls). He seems to have been wiped from their history books but I have asked people and they have verified he did. I've lived in Halifax for the best part of 30 years, falling in and out of different creative outlets to try better myself as I am partially dyspraxic. My love of music started in my teens started with Jimi Hendrix and Punk rock.. It's a been an ever sliding slope to all sorts of music as I believe music has no breed or rules to how good it is!

Q: So what was first introduction to poetry?

KH: I initially started writing poetry in 2012, as a secondary outlet to my music production and Djing. I went to my friend Genevieve Walsh's first ever spoken word night and saw a performer that made me think I could do this. Around about 2014 I had a change of pace in life and fully immersed myself in the art of it.

Q: Whom are your influences?

KH: It would be easy to say I have been influenced by John Cooper Clarke but that is far from the truth. My friend Cayn White whom had been doing the circuit longer than me and making a name for himself in certain poetry circles has been an influence on my work and we sometimes perform together. Another influence is Hip Hop and Rap music, to say I have never had the correct accent to rap on the beat I have considered this music as vital as Punk Rock. Midnight Shelley is another partial influence as if wasn't for her i would not of taken up spoken word in the first place.

Q: What do you write about?

KH: Occasionally I like to write about what is going on in the world around me, namely sometimes politics, my ongoing anger with racist Britain and an outlook to the inner cynicism that makes my town tick. I also take time to write about stuff what I love namely vinyl, music, life itself and whatever tickles my fancy.

Q: Do you consider yourself a poet?

KH: In some circumstances, yes. But I do prefer to be called a Punk poet, as my work isn't always the nicest to read or listen to, plus I LOVE punk rock. i also like the term "cunning-linguist" "word abuser" and my current book title "rebel without a prose"

Q: Do you have any more creative outlets? We hear you make music and draw.

KH: these accusations are true! I've been drawing cartoons ever since I was a child. It has been one of my talent I feel no one can judge, as everyone enjoyed it. I have been making a wide variety of musical projects since 2007 with a laptop. They are widely available on the internet, if you know where to look.

Q: And Finally.. what's next for you?

KH: Inventing the future, then manifesting it.

I am:

My Mum was a punk
My dad a ted
Together they had this child
A bit mixed up in the head
One loved Siouxsie Sioux
The other Elvis P
And that was the conception of me

So while one went to see CRASS
The other collected his giro pass
Now mixing black with white in the eighties wasn't all the rage
But they had this flat capped wearing miscreant, in the color "beige"

I Met God

I met god
In the form of a urinal
Told me he wasn't a DJ
Nor did he spin vinyl
But when we made the connection
His tap into my system felt spinal
He spoke eloquent, his words final:

"Now Keiron,
Recently i haven't heard you pray
And tell me are you practicing to be good, ten times a
day?"

I felt bewildered
And put this voice down to a hallucination
But this damn urinal wouldn't stop
Speaking in this situation!

"Now Keiron,
How far from my flock have you fallen
And if you keep it up
You're on yer way to hell"

"WHO IS THIS?!"

I shouted bluntly at the gutter
Suddenly a tap on the shoulder
Turned out to be a religious nutter..

So It turned out
I didn't have a divine image of a being god
Instead it turned out to be a member of society been
slightly odd
So in this parting note
I'll say believe in what you want to see..
But if I'm in the urinals- don't bother me!!

Confessions Of A Vinyl Addict, Part 1

7 inch
12 inch
45
The look and sound makes me feel alive
Punk, Rock, Reggae and ska
Is the sounds I play from sound systems afar
The wheel is spinning
This man is grinning
The sound of a good record

I Spend money I can't afford
On that one record
Its scratched sometimes
Comes with a hiss
But there isn't a sound I find more authentic than this
So when the needle hits the groove
No time to be rude
No time to be bored
Its a 12 inch
7 inch
180 gram record.

Yes man

I hang around the shop floor all day
Telling people what to do
I like the taste of money
In reality I haven't got a clue
I am a gutless wanker
The suit & tie fits me the best

And if you challenge me
I'll lay your career to rest
A bonafide rat bastard
Who walks on his hind legs
"I hope my boss throws me some crumbs today"

Because I'm the dog who begs
I like to believe I'm a woman or a man
Who always says "YES?"
But given the situation
To run the place
You'd better take a guess

I'd fuck it up discreetly, completely as one would say
And just to cover my downfall
I'd make an employee pay
people call me a cactus
cos in reality I'm just a prick
I live and breathe this company

To the point where you are sick
Just another yes-man
I get the job cos I'm thick
My last name is "fucking head"
And my first name dick!

Rebellion: a Punk Poem

For 4 whole days i went to stay there
Surrounded by studs, docs and spiky hair
This is the place
A mecca where punks young and old meet
Come to see some bands
Or get drunk in the street

Ignore your apparent punk fashion tag
and your right to rebel
Instead meet some of the buckfast drinking crusties
In the corner they dwell
Last year i saw NOFX, The Selector and The English
Dogs too
Drink too much expensive beer
That meant constant trips to the loo

That is my rebellion festival memory
In the blackest of pools
Something I'll never forget
I won't be there this year
But make a bet
They'll be punks, skins and cool people aplenty
Ages ranging from fifty to twenty
So to close this poem here's a phrase often said:
"Long live the rebellion festival, Punk is not dead!"

From Hull to Halifax: A Halifax Love Poem

I was raised in a town
Where memorial plaques
Are placed outside houses
Fridges left on country walks
And a guillotine used as a historical exhibit
But I love my town.

The Hometown of the Big Daddy
Percy Shaw too
We had a hand in Mackintosh's
"From Hull to Halifax The lord shall deliver you"

In the 30s
The Halifax slasher
turned out to be an apparent myth
And the football team we always finished fifth
Welcome to Halifax
The place, not the bank
Occasionally there is friendly folk when there's beer to
be sank

In this place of un-used railways
And green moors far and wide
I do love my town called Halifax
It's an affection i cannot hide.

Confessions Of A Vinyl Addict, pt.2

I love the sound of crackle
I adore the sound of hiss
People thought it was a dying trend
But its a sound I'll never miss

The sound of a new vinyl
Is a sound I love to hear
So pull yourself up real close
And lend me your ear

Now some people like jazz
And others like rock
But the only time I get sad
Is when my records are outta stock

So if you see me playing records
Don't look at me smart or smug
Keep ya CD's and your tapes
Its my preferred kinda drug!

Saturday Night Dive Street

I don't miss the saturdays
around town
Few drinks in, few drinks down
seeing the same old people
each & every week
Oh how i wish to meet someone that bit more unique

I go to three pubs
Then decide to call it a night
then its off to the takeaway
dodging young people
desperate for a fight

The Taxi driver
rips me off
for going half a mile
I try to complain
then he'll explain
he's took me this way for a while

Clock into home
at 3am, the new day is dawning
cos I dared to brave saturday night
and ressurect on Sunday morning

Can't.

You can't do this
dyspraxic child
you have no attention
and you are far too wild
constantly trapped
in your imaginary little Sonic The Hedgehog zone
I think its best
we left you alone

you can't do that
you never made the grades
here's a job or unemployment
dreams for a future in art fades
teenage and introverted
how time has flown
now I just want to be alone

you can't do this- hey
I have things to that need to be said
I'm an adult now
look upon my confidence with dread
former DJ, passed level two English
can drive a car-

Did you dyspraxia,
think i'd make it this far?

Or was it still wanting to keep me
trapped in a no-go zone

with no hopes for the future
destined to be alone

I manage daily
with this blessing, sometimes a curse
where it inspires my creativity
it prays on my mind the worse

So in all walks of life
don't be told "you can't"
when in reality "you can"
and never be afraid when things don't go to plan

for dyspraxia..
you are just one of the many shades of my negative
mind
but i'm older now-
I'd like to leave you behind.

0161

They're coming on a train
to a town near you
bald and brainless
they haven't got a clue
claiming to skinheads
but they're really just dicks
spewing right wing rhetoric
in their rabble of pricks

Forgetting their fondness of curry
or the love of ska
come the weekend a St. George's flag
shall fly from their car
whether its a great British march
or a concert for the R.A.C
the only words are hatred
that separate them from me

"it can't happen here!"
you say to yourself
but watch it will happen
cos they're hazardous to health

their basis is racist- its what they seem to say
and the if the answer isn't violence is your silence
I'm saying 0161!
I want the nazis all GONE!

Bella ciao ciao ciao,
please fuck off now now now!

"So I want all you boneheads
to get the fuck off my streets
retire the braces
and them boots on your feet
before we give some of that

OLD CURBSTOMPING!"

Queen Obscene

You can hang me for treason
if you can give me a reason
why we should onto our queen?

Her views are out of touch
and no cares that much
and the family is pretty obscene

that crown on her head
says "we should be all dead"
fighting wars in her name
sitting on her throne
oh how she does drone
looking for a country to blame

The palace needs money
and people look at me funny

when I say she should fund it herself
cos she is pretty rich
the free loading bitch
and doesn't like to share the wealth!

So god saves the queen
that imaginary being
caring for the upper class
ban the speech
forget the family
and blow it out yer ass!

Alternative "Roses Are Red" verses

Ken is red
Chun-Li blue
if they don't like Street Fighter
they are not the one for you.

Blood is red
black eyes blue
I had a date with Mike Tyson
and lost an ear or two.

I was mislead
by an alcoholic brew
now I'm stuck with a hangover
in the middle with you.

You never did like flowers
or romantic gestures too
I want a divorce this year
I'm taking the dog also from you

Romance is dead
love is too

this is not a love poem
so please just get a clue!

Confessions Of A Pyromaniac

I love the smell of matches
I love to see stuff burn
people think i'm tapped in the head
but when they gonna learn

the smell of fresh turpentine
is a smell I love to taste
so please give me your stuff to burn
don't let em go to waste

some people like sex
others like to steal
but the only thing I like to see naked is a FLAME
cos I believe its got sex appeal.

So if you see me in the streets
don't look at me smart or smug

COS I'LL BURN YA FUCKING HOUSE DOWN!
a certified firebug

90s.

In the 1990s..
we had WWF before WWE
Super Mario Bros.
Sonic 3
Ninja Turtles
Thundercats
Ren & Stimpy, The Rugrats
SNES, NES, Sega Megadrive
John Peel was still alive
Britpop, Hip-Hop, + Grunge
Kurt Cobain, Chuck D
Damon Albarn & Easy E
Michael Jackson went a shade of white
Mike Tyson bit an ear off in a fight
unedited Beano
Desperate Dan
down to the world's worse superhero Bananaman
Oldskool Rave, Ragga Jungle
Mike Patton's Mr. Bungle
Nu Metal, Indie Pop
1999!
then the 2000s came
and everything turned out fin

Dr. Heckle & Mr. Snide

Its sitting at the back
or on the top row
the nefarious kind of being
any performer should know

it needs your attention
for this it can't resist
with its overbearing gob
leaving everyone really pissed

it can be easily shot down
but everyone will ask
why did it come here for?
Just to perform its special task
on occasion it gets ejected
straight out of the door
but sometimes its stays around though
being an unconditional bore

Drunk with power on its own elixir
as it would only seem
the makings of a bonafide twat
we all rightfully deem
But if this certain Dr. Heckle
and Mr. Snide should appear loudly and
starts the same old shit
tell them they have a bus in 10 minutes
and they should be under it!

One Glass

Pouring another glass
of "forget me not"
drowning in endless glass of vodka
and the occasional brandy shot
I'm at my lowest
and all that matter is drink
I don't use it to ease my mind
or have time to think

You see living with this addiction
has caused friction
with all I have love and met
because I have no shame for how drunk
I get
I hate the days when I awake from this Jekyll/Hyde per-
sona

So here's to chewing on an another bottle of ignorant
bliss
as it needs must at times like this
because its just a reminder I'm alone with no future, no
ideals no class.. time to drink the blues away
with one more glass

The Kids Are (Alt) Right

The kids are Alt-Right
brainwashed by fascist shite
"support your country!
Spell it C-U-N-T
and sign up for the racist lobotomy"

But just stop for a moment...
the clothes you wear
the food you eat
and the boots on your feet
where all made by a different race
so don't buy into the Great British disgrace
The fight for "Great" Britain is still been racially
planned thought up by people
whose too ignorant to understand
I don't believe in a front that's national
or a British Nazi Party
I don't want to listen to a bigot
whose probably offended by the colour of a
Smartie
I believe in equality
for you, him, her and me
and ignore those people
who don't want it a reality.

Rocks

I remember when I was a young lad
I was never sort of really bad
but when trouble would come in flocks
my only option was to chuck rocks

I was quite the marksman
could take a kid out sitting on a tree
for each rock thrown
I believed my score would go up
and when i'd finished
i'd be presented with a cup

Didn't matter if it was concrete
or tar
just as long as I could fling it far
never hurt animals
they did nowt to me
just threw them at people
because they where annoying to me!
As I grew older
my pitcher's arm did too
and now I can throw is insults at you
but whenever there's a situation
or the perfect time
I end this rhyme
with extreme caution..
do not confront me
when rocks are in mass proportion!

Degradation Trip

Thoughts full of static
mouth full of dread
no one shall know
what goes on in my head

Thoughts chipping away
and I can't say stop
life is just a ongoing film
and I'm feeling like a prop

Things I love
people that cared
I want all of their worries of me to be spared
Just keep telling yourself
"I'm Ok, I'm not really depressed"
Cause I believe it'd be only weakness
if I confessed

I try to drown my sorrows
turns out they are great swimmers
my life is becoming the light switch
with a bulb that slowly dimmers
trapped in this cycle
this noise about always been OK
just so these thoughts I hope can go away
I can either talk or write
to me that's what really matters
to keep depression away
when happiness shatters

99 DJ Problems

Well its the weekend again
packed the bags full of CD and vinyl
and yet again its pissing down with rain
finally put the bag on my back
and there goes the bus!
No doubt my partners will have something to say about
this.

Finally setting up
its not even 9PM yet and someone drunk is shifting up
asking what's up
seems he wants to know what we play
I point the marquee
and he goes away
judging the way he rolled his eyes
we won't be seeing him again tonight as time flies

Now the music's blaring, we are finally playing to a
packed house!
But there's bloke just staring
he staggers up, and I get preparing..
"excuse me lad, have you got that one song, by that art-
ist?"
confused, I say I haven't exactly got that tune
but hopefully something you like will be on soon?
"Well have you got any Rick Astley?!"
now been i'm playing a setlist of reggae, soul and ska
I tell him no and taking the piss so far
Well finally the night's over
surviving bad requests, records skipping
grumpy bartenders and needles slipping
I saw a bouncer who decided to breakdance
but only broke their nose
serves em right for rocking that pose
I'm 50 quid richer
and this is done
I've got 99 problems
but been a crap DJ isn't one!

Demon Pisshead of Beat Street

Aye up mate!
caught you there
giving me a cold dead stare
this bloke at the end of the bar
thinks of killing me
whilst drinking another jar

He's got the makings of a walking, talking toilet bowl cos
he's never the paper he's not on a roll..
"psycho pisshead, whats he drink?
Stel-la-la lafuckin' Artois" on the rocks
and when opportunity
he'll fall into a complete rage

best believe the rat's outta his cage
Cos you see tonight
he could be Ryu from Street Fighter
or another victim in A&E
so whats it going to be tonight, lamebrain? Lets just wait
and see.

An Experiment In Dentistry and Fear

He can make a smile refrain
shaping you up in his theatre of pain
he doesn't do it for the joy
he does it for the thrill
I'm scared shitless of the man with the dentist drill

All his tools
pull, drill extract
with horrible music playing in the background
trying to distract
you from the horrors of the chair
because he takes pride in his work with a glare
he doesn't do it for the fame
he does it for the thrill
that man in the white coat

with the dentist drill
when its all said and done
you'll come out fine
but when he says "SEE YOU SOON"
there's a chill down my spine
whether its a root canal
extensive surgery
braces
or the occasional thrill..
beware of the man in the white coat
that one with the dentist drill!

Bloodsport

(a poem inspired by the needless brutality of Bull-fighting, a sport still paraded as "entertainment" over in some European countries.)

In a circle of yellow sand
stands a killer dressed so extravagantly grand
to his sides, a crowd that does adore
for the art of murder they came here for

to this would be executioner's centre
stands an animal
frightened, scared and doing no harm
now it is in state of terror, fear and alarm
The crowd cheer "Ole!" and "Toro!"
for each time the bull is stabbed
that is the real sorrow
and soon this animal will be dead
repetitively skewered, and one placed in its head
The feeling of death
is coming oh so near
still this animal will charge
in a state of pain and fear
You see the man in the circle
taunts the animal with a cape of red
and will be considered a hero
when he kills this animal dead
in the name of this sadistic spectator sport
the need for bloodlust is high
and not a thought will be spared
for when this animal will die.
To them its just another bull
ready for the kill
a sickening spectacle in which blood will spill the animal
will die
line up another for the cull..
But in the realm of man Vs. Animal
I cheer for the bull.

Against Apathy

(originally wrote for "firm against apathy")

Here now in Britain
NHS, immigration, and austerity
are an important buzz word
for those who haven't heard
I'm telling you to vote
cos not we'll be in the same boat

constantly complaining, explaining
how we did want this power to be
so its plain to see
pick up that pen
and cast your vote in that box
cos together we can be a powerful movement
when opportunity knocks
You may it doesn't change a lot
but its time for you to give it all you got
time to make a stand
and don't listen to Russell Brand
the power to change this country is your hand
So on that day the 7th of May
Its time for you to have your say
don't be one of those stuck
in the same jaded and unhelpful boat..
only you can change the way the country is run
only when you vote.

21st Century Netjerker

Friendship-family
narrowed down to a TFT screen
gathering of opinion
"social netjerking"

A million faces, identities
all want your absurd view on everything
99% fiction
0% fact
trending topic, status update
celebrities, war, religion, world views, revolution,
humans ALL THE SAME.
Mere personality
becomes celebrity in the blink of an eye format
agreed opinion
narrowed down to a "like"
disagreed opinion- a debate, then blocked. ..is
your friendship
on the digital world
all that's cracked up to be?
*unfriend.

I'm Not Quite...

I'm not quite synched with time and space
my feet never quite touch the ground
my fingers never quite hold
the things I hold

I'm just like you
just plain of out of tune
sort of like a piano
though more like a radio, really
and un-tuned radio..

Like a sock
or a UFO
I'm un-synched with your frequencies
I should know
I'm not quite synched with time and space
my feet never quite touch the ground
am like a crackle you hear
from a un-tuned radio's sound.

Mr. Rich Millionaire

Rich millionaire
wants to close the borders off
rich millionaire
at your poverty he does scoff
rich millionaire
wants to make his country great
rich millionaire
only inspires hate
rich millionaire
belongs somewhere in a dump
rich millionaire
known as Donald Trump

Brexit City Rollers

Farage the fromage
paying homage
to Enoch Powell
a racist poster boy
whom talks from the bowel

Boris Johnson
last name slang for "dick"
an embarrassing cycle riding prick
his hair on his head
leaves not much to be said
they'll be a celebration when they are dead

So you of remained "in" or may have voted
"out
but now no one knows what to do when
Theresa is larking about

Saturday Dive Street, part 2

Take me down
to the Halifax city
where the grass is drugs
and the people are shitty
oh would you please take me home..

cos there's blood on the pavement
piss on the wall
Saturday night dive street
its coming this fall
The nightclub scene
remains obscene
with Spotify DJ's in denial
Its Saturday dive street, a free for all
you'd best run half a mile
The sun's coming up
the vampires of the night sup
on another VK kick
they drink 12 more
and then you know the score
they'll soon be covered in sick
So Saturday night dive street
ends at the crack of dawn
the night club closes
the bouncers pose
and then the weekend is over!

Dump Trump

He's well suited
in his a legion he's recruited
spouting his drivel and bile
"I'll make this country great again"
he says with a liar's smile

America installed him to the white house
on a promise of making things great but
what is great in this debate
when all you do is hate?
They said it couldn't happen
but all the public was fed was seductive
lies
so in this my faith in humanity that bit
much more dies
a new scandal arrives
each and every week
but the "fake news" he spews
can be covered up with money so to
speak
coming to a country near you
a man whose hairpiece could builds
borders too America had to lose
there was no happy medium
enjoy your blonde megalomaniac
whose thoughts rack as tedium

2016

Dead musicians
crazy politicians
EU Referendum

started with a star man
closed with a star wars

Tyskie (A word from our sponsored beverage)

haven't done a ad for nationwide
ain't gonna sell you chips
but when I think of this beverage
the mind just slips
what is this drink that makes me
feel so frisky? That my friends is
my beloved tyskie
its a beer that'll put you in the
driver's seat that one sip will
knock you off your feet
the logo comes with a crown
and I just can't put it down
but too much of the brew can be
risky
so be cautious of that drink
called tyskie
So begone Carling!
retreat to your hiding Stella!
Your taste isn't for this kinda fella
be that beer traitor
drink that stuff that's risky
and crack on with that curious
polish beer codename tyskie!

Puke

I got drunk by myself today
to see if I still feel
I focus on the pint
the only thing that's real

The alcohol fills a hole
that old familiar taste
tried to drink it all away
but I don't remember anything
What have I become?
My sweetest beer
every pint i've known
goes away
in the end
and you could have it all
my empire of ale
I will let you down
I will make you puke.
I wear this crown of drunks
upon my barstool chair
full of drunken thoughts
I cannot repair
beneath the stain of beer
the need to puke goes away
you are somewhere sober
I am still right here
What have I become?
My sweetest beer
every pint i've known
goes away in the end
If I could start again, a million pints away
I wouldn't get hungover by myself
I would get a taxi away!

Reality

Line up the hasbeens!
In the house on the TV screen
we want them debauched
controversial, unfit and unclean

We want to monitor them
just to find out what makes them tick
this year features the semi famous page 3 model
and the soap starring prick
they're here for your entertainment
24/7 a day
hanging onto their celebrity status
selling out the usual way
There's a bloke
who had 1 year of fame
sang his guts out on a pop contest
desperate for more of the same
He's joined by the mouthy youngster
and seasoned mardy sportstar
they all count on your vote
all hoping to get far
After its all over
they'll stranded on an island out in the deep blue
sea claiming this is the closest we'll see them in
reality
Z-lister after Z-lister
talking rubbish
acting bizarre
sometimes offensive
and known to woefully scoff
I don't like reality TV
I think my TV shall remain "off"

20 Years

20 years, a lifetime of tears shed for controversial hero
Now reduced to a marble stone
Here in the cemetery
You can't be alone.

Surrounded by others
Taken before their time
Some young, some old
Some new
But in this place of rest
All that matters is you
A faded Polaroid
A guitar you once did play
I often feel offended when people still say
"You look just like him"
It's a thought that still strikes me as fairly grim
Cos you see I was born a black sheep
from the word go
disregarded over the years by a family
I once did know
we'd always say you'd pull all together
But I am still here
And for that circumstance you are not
But i still leave flowers as a memory on your resting plot.
 I'm a grown man now.
Though I still get occasionally sad
2nd March 1997, the day everything went from good to bad
The final memory of a person
A person I called dad.

This Poem.

(influenced partially by John Cooper Clarke's "I've Fallen In Love With My Wife")

She walks with a blonde hair
Green fringe blur
A poetic mermaid i could care for her
A smile on my face
when my days are blue
This poem is her and it is not for you
A strong fighter for women's rights
She performs her poems under theater spot lights She
likes to cycle
When the days are blue
This is her and it is not for you
We'll meet again
So it seems
under twilight moon beams
I think am in love
could this be true?
This poem is her and it is not for you

A Memoir Of My First Book Of Poetry

This book
for two years has shared the thoughts of me
in the black and blue ink plain to see
in its beauty of love loss
and poems of pyromania and punk

written and bitten
between the lines
of a man aged 29

THE RESPONSE (A Closing note..)

A "poet" called Keiron
has a differing view to me
thought provoking, his words succinct
Though I disagreed
and thought he stinked
But I have no gumption
to express this with decorum because I
am a fool
a drunk
a moron!

For more poetry and connection, please follow me on these links:
http://www.twitter.com/keirohiggspoet
www.writeoutloud.net/profiles/keironhiggins

Lightning Source UK Ltd.
Milton Keynes UK
UKHW041853270119
336313UK00001B/146/P

9 783732 390106